THE FLIGHT OF MY IMAGINATION

POETIC EXPRESSIONS OF A YOUNG HEART

VARDAN SINGH

ISBN 979-888530191-6

I want to dedicate this book to my motherland India,

and my mother, who is my greatest support

Contents

Contents

Foreword

"Poetry is the spontaneous overflow of powerful feelings; it takes its origin from emotions recollected in tranquility." Writing is hard, "I think the hardest thing about writing is writing". It takes immense thought process to give words to the feelings and express through poetry. Even for authors who do it all the time. What should be easy and flowing looks tangled or feeble or overblown at times?

This book by Vardan Singh with the fascinating title "The Flight of My Imagination" is a poetic expressions of an 8 years young boy. Vardan, is an avid reader and keen observer, he has been penning down his thoughts and feelings since a very young age. His writing style is simple and yet the topics he picks have a deep meaning and thoughts. The book provides a wide variety of poems, which showcase the young writers thought process and expressions. His writing cascades his bond with his roots, family and surroundings. The immaculate selection of words in his writing shows a well nurtured and mature mind. The flight of My Imagination is a collection of short poem. Mom-On your birthday is a heartwarming poem, which reflects the emotions and pride Vardan feels for his mom and family. The poem truly makes us feel how important family ties are and allow oneself to feel unique and special. Being myself a mother I can truly correlate with his expressions.

I really feel very proud to have a student like Vardan. His sensitivity, imagination and creativity is spellbound. He is agile, an all-rounder, a multitasker with tons of potential and eager to learn. Hard work never goes unnoticed, I am sure he has wonderful future and life ahead. On behalf of SVIS and his teaching faculty, I wish him all the best for his future endeavours.

Ms. Anita Bisht

Vardan Singh

Acknowledgements

First and foremost, I would like to thank God for giving me the skill to write stories and poems. I would also like to thank my nation, India (land of creativity and oldest civilisation). I am proud of our ancient sages and the knowledge that they acquired centuries before. I hope I will get some of their wisdom that I can use for the betterment of humanity in future.

I want to thank my grandparents – Mr Ram Singh and Mr Balkar Singh, for always inspiring me to achieve big goals and do something better for society. My loving grandmothers – Smt. Krishna and Smt. Shakuntla, whose dosage of unconditional love always fills my heart with happiness.

My super awesome dad – Mr Dal Singh, a very calm and light-hearted man. He always wears a bright smile on his face and bears strength in his arms. He teaches me how to spread my wings while my legs stay rooted to the ground. I always enjoy wrestling with my dad, which makes me feel energetic. Thanks, Dad!!

Now comes the most important and valuable person of my life, my darling mom – Dr Mukta Sandhu. She is the one who has done a lot to lighting the spark of creativity in me. She is the one who introduced me to story formation. I wrote my first unpublished book when I was 3 years old. Since then, she inspired me to write more. Her smile while listening to my stories encouraged me, and gradually, I started writing effortlessly. I truly acknowledge her love, support and encouragement. I LOVE YOU, MOM, A LOT!!!!

Venayak Singh – my creative, super talented and intelligent big brother. Thanks a lot for the fun we always had. He helps me a lot especially sharing his wisdom and knowledge with me. I love talking to him, and he contributed a lot to creating interest in reading books. Because of him, I have finished 'The Kane Chronicles' series, which is beyond my level. Thanks, my great brother!!!

Next, I want to express my sincere gratitude to my principal – Mrs Nita Arora, for her kindness and loving nature. Finally, I want to thank all my teachers since preschool—Ms Julie, Ms Nancy, Ms Little, Mrs Manisha Bajaj, Mrs Rashmi Malik and Mrs Anita Bisht for nurturing and teaching me. Without your contribution, I wouldn't be able to do what I'm doing today. I appreciate your kindness and support in my journey.

I want to extend my thanks to Ms Manisha G. Bhise – founder of Gappa Stories & More for children, who introduced me to the process of poetry writing.

How can I forget my other family members and friends - you all are a large part of my journey. I am really thankful for your love, care, support and continuous encouragement.

1. Haiku Collections

High speed of football
And the energy involved
Brings fun on the ground

Soccer is so fun
Even Sweat is rewarding
And worth playing it

A strong and green tree
Peaceful and standing upright
In front of our house

Blessings of my life
More precious than anything
Are my mom and dad

Few tiny red ants
Moving freely near mountains
Taking food up Hill

2. India: My Nation, My Pride

India got its independence on 15 August 1947
Thanks to our freedom fighters,
That made our life feel like heaven
They fought a long battle with Britishers

Our brave soldiers turned their army into the sand
And took control of their hand
We finally got freedom, and it was nice
But we had to pay a heavy price.

So many people had casualties,
It was as bad as a swarm of angry bees.
Their sacrifice should not go in vain,
They gave us freedom, which is a vast gain.

You see,
We are all now free.
I salute the soldiers for their sacrifice
Now it's our turn to make our country wise.

3. Who am I?

My name is Vardan.
I am a boy,
Not anyone's toy.

I'm in 3rd grade,
And I do some trade.
My hobbies are writing poems and reading books,
And I have great looks.

I desire to win,
But when I lose, it all goes to the bin.
Sometimes I fail, and that is fine
After all; every feeling is mine

Mukta is the name of my mother
Venayak is the name of my brother
My father's name is Dal Singh
He looks like a king
We live in Delhi
Where we eat lots of jellies…

4. Mom - on your Birthday

Dear mom, this is your day
You always lead the way
You are very caring
Also, super daring.

You never leave me alone.
You always sweep me into your zone.
I stick to you like glue,
And you never flew.

Your target is as sharp as a nail,
And you never let anyone fail.
You never let me lose hope;
Instead, you always show me how to cope.

Mom, you are my pride,
You are my guide.
Your love is unparallel to any other.
You are the best person ever.

May your happiness always rise higher,
And your rays shine brighter than fire.
You are greater than the whole universe combine;
To me, you are just divine.

My mom is the best,
Like a safe, strong chest.
You are as tough as leather,
Most importantly, you are my mother.

5. Happy Birthday, Dad

Happy Birthday, Dad!
Your presence makes me glad.
It makes me happy,
Not nappy.

Playing with you is fun,
Because you are as fast as a shot of a gun.
I wish our love never ends,
Or bends.

You are the best,
You play with me without rest.
I never see you sad,
Happy birthday, Dad.

6. My Loving Family

My family is very caring;
they are very supportive.
My family is better than gold,
I don't know how it stays so bold.

My mother is very peaceful,
And beautiful.

I love her a lot as she is awesome,
her presence makes my life blossom.
In my tiny heart,
she holds a special part.

I like playing with my brother,
I can never replace him with another.
His name is Venayak,
Always busy in technology hack
He is very nice
And gives me the best advice.

My father is never wrong;
He always stays so strong.
You see, my family is the best,
We have faced life's test.

7. Friends

Friends are great,
they are our best mates.

When we are sad,
friends help us not to feel bad.

When we want to play out,
we just need to shout.

While we talk to our friends,
they make our bad feelings end.

Best friends are like stars,
they remove our saddest scars.

Friendship is always sweet compatibility,
We need to maintain it with the highest responsibility.

8. My Prayer on the Environment Day

I see a beautiful tree
standing in front of me
it always stays so long;
also, it remains so strong.

it looks so peaceful
and it is very beautiful
if you save a tree now
they will make you say, "wow."
we will clean our earth today
To save the day.

On this Environment Day
I want you all to pray
to bless our mother earth
as it gave us birth
she needs us to make it clean
I wish it would always stay green.

9. Solar System

Mercury is the closest to the Sun
that must be so much fun.
Venus is so shiny and bright;
Like a diamond, it delights.

The earth is the only planet that has life.
That's why it keeps us alive.
Mars has the longest dust storm
That makes it so strong.

Jupiter has the shortest day;
I wonder what is there today?
Saturn has a beautiful ring,
which makes it appear like a king.

Uranus rotates on its sides,
It may have a bumpy ride.
Neptune is very cold,
There is no life it can hold.

We have the sun, which is only one,
with this, our solar system is done.

10. Sunflower

The sunflower is my favourite flower;
It looks like it has lots of power
When it is young, it always faces the Sun
That sounds so much fun.

Big ones face the east,
Just like the beast.
Its botanical name is Helianthus Annuus,
In the whole world, it is very famous.
Not all sunflowers are yellow,
red, and purple, are it's a unique fellow.

It can range in various heights;
good thing they never bite.
The tallest sunflower is 30 feet tall
but it never falls.

Do you know
it increases our health power?
And our bodies empower.
The sunflower can self-pollinate,
Lucky flower travels to space.
I love sunflowers,
and they are my favourite flowers.

11. Save Them!

If there is no sun
it won't be fun
life will pop and stop.

Without the sun,
we cannot run.
And if there is no ice,
it won't be nice,
As it can kill the polar bear,
And that will be unfair.

We all need to stop global warming
For years our Earth has been suffering,
Therefore, it's now or never
The polar bear has to live forever.

Please don't cut the trees,
This way, we are cutting the home of bees.
We should not break the link
"You are a gem!" the animals will think

12. My Mischievous Memory

One day, I saw my mom light a match,
after she was done, I gave it a snatch.
The match lit and was about to burn my hand,
lucky for me, I was wearing a band.
It burned down the whole Temple
And I wondered how it would be reassembled.

The other day I got a mouse,
And put in the house.
I scared my brother to death,
thinking something was wrong with his health.

Once I poured water on my dad's hand
along with some sand.
Then I placed a buzzing sound of a mosquito near his ear;
my brother gave me thumbs up and a cheer.
After that, he placed a hand on his face;
he looked like he came from space.

13. My Dream House

If I had a mansion,
it would be big.
There would be a farm,
but no pigs.

It's colour will be bright
like white.
It would be fun
to live in it
not bad, a bit.

It would have food,
which is very good.
It would have a car
for travelling far.

My family will live in my house,
but there will be no mouse.
It would be the best home,
packed with love and life in our dome...

14. My Visit to Rashtrapati Bhavan

We visited Rashtrapati Bhavan
before Covid hit us hard
And we got inside
Our houses…

I went with my brother
mother and father.
It was legendary.
Can you believe it?
We saw all the rooms
There were hundreds of them.

That is a huge mansion
Where our
respected President resides.
My favourite room was the guest room
The whole building is guarded
by thousands of guards.

I want this pandemic to go away soon
So that I can visit it again …

15. My Weird Dream

Once I saw three men
dressed as hens.
Carrying honey
to earn some money.

They had a funny-looking beard,
And were looking very weird.
One tripped on a rock,
He froze like an ice block.

No one saw them except me,
They turned into small bees,
After that, I saw one was there,
But then it flew, God knows where.

I was in a forest,
The animal kingdom chorused.
Then I saw the light beam,
And realised it was all a dream.

16. Wacky Tribute to Dr Suess

When I woke up, I saw a ball on the wall.
Why was it there at all?
Then, I looked out the window,
and said, "oh my God!"
I saw three more wacky things,
waiting for me.
Apples growing on a mango tree,
everything was so free.

I saw a worm crawling after a bird.
I thought I was being a nerd.
The ground was filled with the grout
I was about to pass out.
I went to school,
everything was out of the rule.
I saw a lady, who was shady.
I was filled with fear.
Then she said, "you are the only wacky person here."

I went to school and said,
"Miss Grass, two things are wrong in your class."
She took me out of her class by pulling my glass.
I heard a voice, saying
Wake up, Boys…
Or I will take your toys...

17. When I Saw an Alien

I saw an alien,
his name was Gallian.

He was very nice,
and as fast as mice.

Playing with him was fun,
because he could get any Nerf gun.

We had epic nerf fights,
and sometimes we played with kites.

He had a fantastic suit
and was dressed to the boot

He made many memes
but that was all in my dreams.

18. If I have Power

If I have the power
It will be of water

I can control the sea
everyone will need me

but I will do no harm
instead, I will help the farm

I will be in every house
Turning everyone wise

the world will be happy
because of me.

19. How Do I Write Poems?

Sometimes I wonder
why thoughts come to me like thunder?
I try to put them down on paper with the help of a pencil,
using all my potential.

After writing, I feel so relaxed,
And it feels like being waxed.
There is my writing diary
That I always carry.

To me, writing poems are the best
because I write them without any rest.
Now, I am done with another poem,
That's how I write my poems…

20. Bear with a Crown

There was a bear,
With a lot of fear
It was brown;
and it had a crown.

Wait, it was turning red,
From toe to head,
Then blue,
After that, it flew.

I caught it in time,
The police investigated but found no crime.
They said it was a magical bear
with a lot of hair.

Someone will get it bail,
please don't put it in jail.

It was wearing a mask of green
I felt the need to intervene.
So, I gave it food,
and feel very good.

21. Super Heroes Lost their Powers

If superheroes lost their powers,
Then it will be like a broken flower.

Captain America turned mad,
Everyone thought he was bad.

Iron man lost his suit,
So, he gave a big hoot.

Hulk lost his strength and length.
Batman lost his wealth,
Also, doesn't have a great heart.

I hope they get their powers back
because I did the hack.

22. God of Laser

Last Monday when
I was playing Atlas with my friend,
I saw an object
flying outside our classroom.
I thought it was a UFO,
but then it broke our window.
We saw a witch.

She was as ugly as a chicken,
She looked as cruel as a feral hag,
She put a magical spell on my friend,

Because he was laughing at her.
She turned him into a frog.
I felt some power rushing
through my spinal cord,
Then, I got a laser sword.

My skin was turning into a laser,
Finally, I slashed her to pieces.
I caught her wand and set a spell,

As a result
I got my friend back again.
And I realise that
I am a God of the laser.

23. I Miss My School Days

School days are happy
Home days are nappy

I want friends to meet
talking with them will be a treat

We will rock
and play with chalk

I hope when we will race
I will get first place.

This coronavirus is not cool.
I wish to go back to school.

24. COVID 19

I don't like COVID-19,
it is mean.
It doesn't let me play
with my friends.

And let's all pray
to stop Covid today
by washing our hands,
without feeling bad

I feel sad
When I can't go outside.
But staying in our home
we will fight this.

And I am sure
Humans will win
Against this pandemic.

25. Tender Pain

When the blood came,
It hurt like a flame.
It is a gift to our body,
it's kind of goody.
But when it came out,
it takes the water out of us like a drought.

Blood is an important thing.
But when it comes out,
I feel the sting.
When the cut heals,
you don't know how it feels.
It gives me relief,
And evaporates my grief.

26. A Story

Robbie and Molly were their names;
they were playing Nerf war
in the backyard.

Then they saw a girl
Named Britney,
who injured her leg.
So, she was in a wheelchair.

On that sunny day,
when the girl-next-door
asked them to play,
Robbie and Molly agreed.
But her wheelchair broke down.

Robbie Molly and their dad
made a wheelchair for the day.
They played happily after again.

27. Among Us

My favourite video game is among us,
I sometimes play it on the bus.
It is so funny
I can't say it is done.

It is so much fun to play,
I am sure to say
it is the best game ever
I can't say, "no, never."

I play like a boss,
But sometimes, I'm at a loss.
I play it for 30 minutes a day,
And then I stay away.
It can hurt my eye
That's why...

28. Fox in the Box

There was once a box
which acted like a fox
it was very clever,
but light as a feather.
A human being picked it up
and shoved it into a pair of socks

29. An Old Book

I feel very gloomy,
please read me.
I will be your great roomy,
You will surely like me.

I will be loveable
You know …
I am very valuable
Please don't throw.

I can provide you knowledge,
which is very rare.
And you will acknowledge,
I need some care.

Nobody likes me as I am old,
But always remember old is gold.

30. When I Have Nothing to Write

What should I write?
Nothing is in sight!

Should I write a book
about the earth that shook?

Should I write about a spider
Or a rider?

A person who could flee
Or a bee?

Should I write about a rat
Or a hat?

Don't be afraid…
That's how poems are made.

Afterword

As a storyteller I always use a poem or a song to begin and end my session, it adds a rhythm and energy to the entire event and helps me break-the-ice with an unknown audience. I had seen the benefits of a rhyme to initiate curiosity and that is how I started my "Pen-a-Poem" session for children from March 2021. After completing 30 sessions since then and helping almost 100 aspiring poets to pen their thoughts, little did I know that one of them would publish a book of his own.

Vardan was one of my student, a calm, observant and curious boy who was stuck by the poetry-writing bug. His reading habit never kept him out of words and his imaginative juices flowed as we touched upon a Haiku or a Limerick or Free Verse. Whatever kind of poem he write, he made sure it had a his own unique touch. During one such session, I remember, I explained the ways to write a "Free Verse" poem and gave them an impromptu object to write a poem. There was an amazon carton laying at his house and bingo, Vardan had the "Fox in the Box" poem written in no time. I was amazed by the sheer talent and imagination he portrayed while writing a poem for his Father on "Father's Day" too.

Wishing him best wishes and promising journey as a poet forever! If you want your children to pen their thoughts too in a poetry form, do grab this book and let Vardan inspire his peers positively all over.

Manisha Bhise

(Founder Gappa Stories & More)

www.ingramcontent.com/pod-product-compliance
Lightning Source LLC
Chambersburg PA
CBHW040113150726